EASY SPANISH CROSSWORD PUZZLES

Jane Burnett

Printed on recyclable paper

PASSPORT BOOKS
a division of *NTC Publishing Group*
Lincolnwood, Illinois USA

1995 Printing

Published by Passport Books, a division of NTC Publishing Group.
© 1985, 1973 by NTC Publishing Group, 4255 West Touhy Avenue.
Lincolnwood (Chicago), Illinois 60646-1975 U.S.A.
Manufactured in the United States of America.

4 5 6 7 8 9 VP 9 8

INTRODUCTION

Bilingual crossword puzzles are a highly effective *and* fun technique for learning or reviewing vocabulary in a foreign language. The crossword puzzles in *Easy Spanish Crossword Puzzles* can both enhance your command of vocabulary and increase your "feel" for the Spanish language in general.

The puzzles in this book offer another advantage. Each one is based on a specific topic related to the activities and concerns of daily life. Subjects such as "The House," "Clothing," and "Food" are important language areas for the beginner to master. The topic arrangement of *Easy Spanish Crossword Puzzles* allows you to concentrate on vocabulary of interest and importance to you.

Units in this book have been arranged according to difficulty in three sections. *Easy Spanish Crossword Puzzles* begins with simple English-to-Spanish puzzles (pages 4–17), followed by Spanish-to-English puzzles (pages 18–35). The more challenging Spanish-to-Spanish puzzles are found in the last third of the book. Although each of these sections offers a greater challenge than the one before it, the book as a whole was conceived for *your* pleasure—no matter what your level of Spanish-language expertise. To check your answers, complete vocabulary lists of all words used and a comprehensive Answer Key have been provided.

NUMBERS

HORIZONTALES:

1. Fourteen
6. To unite
7. He
9. To fall
10. Ninth
13. Fowl
16. Sixty

VERTICALES:

1. Hundreds
2. You (fam.)
3. Eleven
4. You laugh (pl.)
5. I believe
8. It
11. You see (fam.) (subj.)
12. One (fem.)
14. He sees
15. On

INFINITIVES

HORIZONTALES:

1. To speak
6. To fall
8. He may use (subj.)
9. To roast
10. To go
11. To give
13. To go
14. To open

VERTICALES:

2. To accuse
3. To base
4. To read
5. Infinitive ending
7. To enclose
9. To inherit
12. To hear

WATER

HORIZONTALES:

3. It
4. Ocean
8. Estuary (pl.)
   (two wds.)
10. Faith
11. Negative
12. Ventilation
13. Yacht
15. Lake
16. To go

VERTICALES:

1. Gulf
2. Month
3. They praise
5. To fall
6. Brook
7. Neither, nor
9. To be accustomed
14. Obj. of "tu"

MORE NUMBERS

HORIZONTALES:

1. Twenty-two
5. One
6. Twelve
7. This
9. From
10. One
12. Ditto (abbr.)
14. Thirteen (pl.)
16. Half
17. Zero
18. Thousand
20. Hundred
21. Gold

VERTICALES:

1. Twentieth
2. Ninety
3. Twelfth
4. Eleven
8. You (fam.)
11. Order (noun)
13. I gave
15. Alone
19. To go

ANIMALS

HORIZONTALES:

1. Horse
5. Stroke (noun)
7. To give
9. Echo
10. I bind
12. Tracks, trails
13. Handle (noun)

VERTICALES:

1. Lamb
2. Donkey (pl.)
3. The (fem. pl.)
4. Eye
6. Cats
8. Here
10. Altar
11. Bear (fem.)

THE CALENDAR

HORIZONTALES:

1. Wednesday
7. One
8. Aunt
9. Axle
11. Your (pl.)
12. Six
13. Under (prep.)
14. I see
16. Winter
19. Postscript (abbr.)
20. South American (abbr.)

VERTICALES:

1. Tuesday
2. Season
3. You eat (fam.)
4. Monday
5. In
6. Saturday
10. Thursday
13. They are
15. Epoch, age
16. Ditto (abbr.)
17. She goes
18. Bishop (abbr.)

COLORS

HORIZONTALES:

1. Orange
5. See
7. Here
10. Emerald
14. Gray
15. On
16. From
18. Tall
20. Is
21. Long
22. Autumn
24. So
25. Bear

VERTICALES:

2. August (abbr.)
3. Yellow
4. White
5. Green
6. Is
8. Auburn, chestnut
9. To the
11. Milligram (abbr.)
12. Was
13. From
17. Plural ending
19. Diamonds (in cards)
22. To you (fam. pl.)
23. Obj. pronoun (fam.)

FOOD

HORIZONTALES:

1. Dining rooms
6. To roast
7. Orange
9. You may laugh
12. Fig
13. Decoration
14. Or
15. To the (masc.)
16. I
19. The (masc.)
21. Clear soup
     (two wds.)

VERTICALES:

1. Shrimp (pl.)
2. To you (fam. pl.)
3. Apple
4. He was
5. Bear (fem.)
8. Juice
10. To go
11. Sauce
12. Today
17. She prays
18. Grape
20. It

AT THE BANK

HORIZONTALES:

1. Credit
7. Bulls
8. Ox less than two years old
9. To pay
11. To use
13. Yes
14. Plural ending
16. Bank

VERTICALES:

1. Checks
2. Station, stopover
3. Dollar
4. To go
5. All (fem.)
6. To you (fam. pl.)
10. Rich
12. Your Holiness (abbr.)
15. On

IRREGULAR VERBS

HORIZONTALES:

1. I have (aux.)
2. You see
5. You give (fam.)
6. To count
8. There is, are
9. *So
10. Laugh (command)
11. I believed
13. I heard

VERTICALES:

1. You have (aux.)
2. They go
3. To be
4. He would say (cond. tense)
5. I give
6. To fall
7. *So
12. To go

*Only words not irr. verbs

BUSINESS

1		2		3	4	5
	■		■	6		
7	8		■		■	■
9			10		■	11
	■	■	12		13	
14	15	16				
17			■	18		

HORIZONTALES:

1. Credit
6. My (pl.)
7. Thousand
9. Lawn, pasture
12. Maple tree
14. Business affairs
17. Odd, uneven
18. Wing

VERTICALES:

1. They buy
2. She
3. Be important
4. To you (fam.)
5. To you (fam. pl.)
8. To go
10. You give (pl.)
11. It weighs
13. Cabbage
15. Under
16. One

THE GARDEN

<table>
<tr><td></td><td>1</td><td>2</td><td>3</td><td></td><td>4</td><td></td></tr>
</table>

HORIZONTALES:	VERTICALES:
1. Garden	1. Hyacinth
5. Shovel	2. To the (two wds.)
6. Perhaps	3. Rakes
8. If	4. Ditto (abbr.)
9. She gives	5. Promenade, walk
10. In	7. Sheaf (grain)
11. Root	9. I gave
13. Others (masc.)	12. So
14. Or	
15. Without	

THE OPERA

HORIZONTALES:

1. Obj. pronoun
3. Tub
6. Usher
7. I know
8. Yes
9. Chords
12. Or
13. He praises
14. Your
15. It has (aux.)

VERTICALES:

1. Musicians
2. Axle
3. Theaters
4. To go
5. Artist
8. South American (abbr.)
10. He
11. He gives

MACHINES

HORIZONTALES:

1. Garages

4. Machine

7. Avenue (abbr.)

8. You (fam.)

9. Brake

12. Us

VERTICALES:

2. To the (two wds.)

3. Water

4. Engine

5. Four (Rom. Num.)

6. Cars

9. Railroad (abbr.)

10. On

11. Negative

LA ESCUELA

HORIZONTALES:

1. Escuela
5. Arriba
7. Caballo
9. Estado de los E.U.
12. Visto
13. Osar
14. América del Sur (abrev.)
15. Entrada
16. Negocio
18. Maestros
20. Libros

VERTICALES:

1. Estudiante
2. Corazón
3. Exclamación
4. Pérdida
5. Usar
6. Lápiz
8. Libro para escuela
10. Un color
11. De ella
16. Escritorio
17. Ud. pregunta
19. Editor (abrev.)

DENTRO DE LA CASA

HORIZONTALES:

1. Muebles
7. Es
8. Fusible
10. Camas
12. Alfombras
14. Nosotros
15. Precio
17. Catre
18. Luz
19. Mucho
20. Corriente Alterna (abrev.)
21. Modo
22. Silla
25. Calle (abrev.)
26. Cielo

VERTICALES:

1. Hogar
2. Nos
3. Si
4. Baños
5. Usar
6. Secoya
9. Tal
11. Sofá
12. Equipo
13. Obtener
16. Rico
17. Reloj
23. Como
24. Lo

NUMEROS

HORIZONTALES:

1. Cincuenta y cuatro
7. Sobre
8. Lo
9. Ochenta
10. Diez (sufijo)
11. Treinta
13. Solamente
15. Opuesto de sí
16. Siete (pl.)
18. Seis (núm. rom.)
19. Terminación (de
    núm. ord.)
20. Sexto
21. El

VERTICALES:

1. Cuarenta y uno
2. Dentro de
3. Veintiséis
4. Cifra (abrev.)
5. Otro
6. Rayo
12. Décimo
14. Opuesto de sí
17. Ella
18. Seis (núm. rom.)

ADJETIVOS

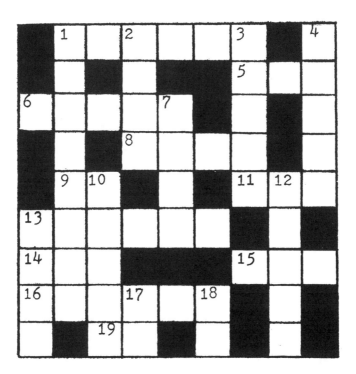

HORIZONTALES:

1. Bonito
5. Viejo
6. Siete
8. Mediodía
9. América del Sur (abrev.)
11. Obtener
13. Más fácil
14. Hormiga
15. Mojado
16. Fuerte
19. O

VERTICALES:

1. Agradable
2. Liso
3. Joven
4. Adulto
7. Ninguno
10. Estrella (prefijo)
12. Cada
13. Oriente
17. O
18. Ir

EL CUERPO

HORIZONTALES:

1. Hombros
9. Riñón
10. Lo
11. Arriba
12. Edad
13. Estar
15. Canción de cuna
19. Dedo del pie
20. Izquierdo
22. Es (contracción)
23. Nariz
24. Tú pareces
26. Muñeca

VERTICALES:

1. Cráneo
2. Cadera
3. En descubierto (abrev.)
4. Inhábil
5. Pierna
6. Tinte
7. Costilla
8. Paso
14. Ojos
16. Decir
17. Perder
18. Sangre
21. Sentir
22. Es
25. Mi

EL TIEMPO

HORIZONTALES:

1. Luz del sol
6. A
7. Símbolo para sodio
9. Más ruidoso
11. Peor
12. De
14. Agüero
15. Cielo
17. Lluvia
20. Luna
21. Enfado
22. Sudoeste (abrev.)
23. Dejar

VERTICALES:

1. Así
2. Tempestuoso
3. Casa
4. Nornordeste (abrev.)
5. Tierra
8. Nube
9. Mirar
10. Guarida
13. Fahrenheit (abrev.)
15. Nieve
16. Lodo
18. Afligir
19. Red
20. Predicción del tiempo
    (más nieve, por ejemplo)
    (abrev.)

EL CORREO

HORIZONTALES:

1. Combustible
4. Rojo
6. Carteros
7. Giro postal (abrev.)
8. Avenida (abrev.)
9. Ceniza
10. Hecho
11. Lo
12. Arriba
13. Césped
14. De
16. Contador Público
     (abrev.)
18. Apartado Aéreo
     (abrev.)
19. Ser
20. Carta
21. Diez
22. Sudeste (abrev.)

VERTICALES:

1. Ir
2. Como
3. Estampilla
4. Leer
5. Sobres
6. Franqueo
7. Correo
12. Tío
14. Gordo
15. Más
17. Pluma
19. Por

VERDE

HORIZONTALES:

1. Verde
4. Arbol
6. Llevar
7. Musgo
10. Alférez (abrev.)
11. Remo
12. Agil
14. O
15. Seis (núm. rom.)
18. Suceso
21. Siete
22. Deber
24. Finca

VERTICALES:

1. Hierba
2. Rojo
3. Salvo error (abrev.)
4. Diez
5. Como
6. Hojas
7. Mayo
8. O
9. Arbol siempre verde
11. O
13. Pinos
16. Tengo (contracción)
17. Raíz
19. Víspera
20. Explosivo (abrev.)
23. Nosotros

EL ASUETO

HORIZONTALES:

1. Vacaciones
8. Pasado
9. Usar los remos
10. Juego
11. Aviso
12. Semestre
13. Fermenta
16. Verdadero
18. Dos (prefijo)
19. Opuesto de sí
21. Lo
22. En
23. Taladro
26. Maleta
27. Pescar

VERTICALES:

1. Vagabundos
2. El que acampa
3. Edad
4. A
5. Orden
6. Negativo
7. Natación
11. A
14. Nosotros
15. Zarpa
17. Teniente (abrev.)
18. Bote
20. O
24. Si
25. Cincuenta y uno
(núm. rom.)

MEDICO

HORIZONTALES:

1. Casualidades
7. Enfermera (abrev.)
8. Lo
9. Incendiar
11. El que hace
13. Usar
14. Enjuagar
15. Tos
19. Tener
20. Citó
22. Terminación
      plural
23. Médico

VERTICALES:

1. Ambulancia
2. Curar
3. Médico (abrev.)
4. Terminación
5. Ata
6. Camilla
10. Nos
12. Sobre
15. Catre
16. Debido
17. Desatar
18. Herido
21. Es

LOS DEPORTES

HORIZONTALES:

1. Jugando al golf
6. Ganó
7. Remo
8. De
9. Plural (abrev.)
10. Doce pulgadas (abrev.)
11. Red
13. Sustituto (abrev.)
14. Jugar
15. En
16. Manera de pescar
18. Hijo
19. Nuestro
20. Vuelta completa
    de la pista
22. Sobre
23. Mi

VERTICALES:

1. Meta
2. En
3. Un juego popular
4. Negativo
5. Juego
9. Pagado (abrev.)
10. Lleno
11. Opuesto de sí
12. Tenis
13. Deporte
15. Orden de (abrev.)
16. También
17. Correr
18. Espía
21. Antes del mediodía
    (abrev.)

SPANISH/ENGLISH 29

LA BODA

HORIZONTALES:

1. Flores
6. Novia
8. Llevaron
9. Estesudeste (abrev.)
11. Tímido
12. Hacer
14. O
15. Anillo
17. Hombre
18. Margen
19. Cosa
21. Canción
22. Voy
23. Nosotros
24. Mayo

VERTICALES:

1. Francés (abrev.)
2. Lirio
3. Poema
4. Boda
5. Centeno
6. Canastas
7. Ceremonia
10. Así
13. Sobre
15. Sonó
16. Novio
17. Mío
20. Cómo

ANIMALES SALVAJES

HORIZONTALES:

1. Elefantes
7. Exclamación
8. Monedas
10. Arriba
11. Parque zoológico
13. Sud América (abrev.)
14. Hiena
15. Acorralar
17. Apuestas
19. Olor
20. Así
21. Felpudo
23. ¡Socorro! (abrev.)
24. Fuera

VERTICALES:

2. Leopardo
3. Pantera
4. Antes del mediodía
   (abrev.)
5. A
6. Tímido
8. Costumbres
9. Bien cocido
11. Cebra
12. Avenas
16. Largos períodos de
    tiempo
18. Blando
21. Mi
22. A

AMARILLO

HORIZONTALES:

1. Descubrimiento
7. Mazorca
8. Cervato
9. Galón (abrev.)
10. Estar
11. Sobre
13. Voy
14. Hacer
15. Amarillo
17. Lo
18. Una isla cerca de Java
19. Limón
22. Dentista (abrev.)
23. Mayor (abrev.)
24. Curioso

VERTICALES:

1. Narcisos
2. Coser
3. Canario
4. O
5. Borde
6. Amarillento
10. Bulbo
12. Elector
13. Oro
16. Señora
20. En
21. Opuesto de sí

EL RANCHO

HORIZONTALES:

1. Ganadero
8. En
9. Oreja
10. ¡Jo!
11. En
12. Avena
13. Herraje de sillero
15. Es
16. Oeste
18. Apartado Aéreo (abrev.)
19. Mí
20. A
21. Ultra (prefijo)
22. Así
23. Rancho
25. Trabaja

VERTICALES:

1. Vacas
2. Un
3. Guarda
4. Ciudad de E.U.(abrev.)
5. Terminación comparativa
6. Montón de heno (2 palabras)
7. No
11. Idiota
12. Mineral en bruto
14. Oveja
17. A
18. Arado
19. Signo
21. Nos
24. Como

VAMOS DE COMPRAS

HORIZONTALES:

1. Zapatería (2 palabras)
8. Sastre
9. Limones
10. Compañía (abrev.)
11. Veterinario (abrev.)
12. En
14. América del Sur (abrev.)
15. Suela de un zapato
17. En
18. Bebida del verano
19. Material sintético
20. Terminación comparativa
21. Negocio
22. Sesión

VERTICALES:

1. Medias
2. ¡Ja!
3. Oleo
4. Ascensores
5. Algunos
6. Trota
7. Revendió
13. Aguja
14. Ventas
16. Hecho de roble
21. Hacer

LOS PAISES

HORIZONTALES:

1. América
6. Tratar
7. Cultivar
10. Sotavento
11. País de América
    del Sur
13. Diez (núm. rom.)
14. Seis (núm. rom.)
15. País de América del
    Norte
17. En
18. Capital de Perú
20. Vago
22. Por
23. Un
24. Imitar
25. Dentro de

VERTICALES:

1. Península oriental
2. Mi
3. Si
4. Llamar
5. Están
8. Mexicano
9. Tokío está allí
12. Península europea
15. Habana está allí
16. Ciudad de Alaska
19. Hombre
21. Arriba
22. Ser

AVIACION

HORIZONTALES:

1. Aviones
6. Hijo
7. Billete
8. Raro
10. Obedecer
12. La forma de oxígeno que combina (prefijo)
13. Clase de avión
14. Un
16. Terminación plural
17. El mundo, por ejemplo
20. Diez
22. Atún
23. Juguete
24. Semestre

VERTICALES:

1. Avión de retro-propulsión
2. Cohete
3. Astropiloto
4. Opuesto de sí
5. Entrada
9. Hacha
11. Acosar
14. Altura (abrev.)
15. Lo
18. Nornordeste (abrev.)
19. Oreja
21. Negativo

VAMOS A ARREGLARNOS

HORIZONTALES:

1. El que corta el pelo
5. Persona que cuida
   las uñas
9. A el
10. Artículo (pl.)
13. Destrucción
16. Rasuradas
19. Hacer crespo el pelo
20. Buena
21. Andar
22. Bajar
23. Desde

VERTICALES:

1. Peinado
2. Provechoso
4. Estuario
6. A el
7. Cercena
8. El que usa
11. El friccionar el cuerpo
12. Se usa para peinar
    el pelo
14. Idem (latín) (abrev.)
15. América del Norte
    en inglés (abrev.)
17. No caliente
18. Elevar
20. Ferrocarril (abrev.)

LA FAMILIA

HORIZONTALES:

1. Esposo de la madre
5. Hermana del padre
   o madre
7. Reir (subj.)
8. Existir
10. Andar
11. Un metal
12. Pronombre
13. Nosotros
15. Quiero
16. Niño de los padres
17. Agua caliente y
    jabón
18. Lateral
20. Algo
22. Mayo, por ejemplo
23. Pronombre neutro
24. Opuesto de sí

VERTICALES:

1. Hija de la tía
2. Brisa
3. Dona, regala
4. Marido
5. Obrar
6. No arriba
9. Ese hombre
13. Muchachos
14. Se usa para ver
16. Fabrica
19. Metal amarillo
21. A él

LA CIUDAD

HORIZONTALES:

1. Vía
7. Usar los ojos
9. Opuesto de no
11. Señor (abrev.)
12. Manzana (de casas)
14. Hacia
15. Fundamento
16. Prefijo que cambia activo a "no" activo
17. Municipio
18. Avenida (abrev.)
19. Están
21. Obispo (abrev.)
23. Cerro pequeño
25. Conjunción
26. Parque municipal

VERTICALES:

2. Avenida (abrev.)
3. Tienda
4. Andar
5. Pronombre
6. Paradero de tren
8. Coche de trole
10. Imperativo de "raer"
11. Secretaría (abrev.)
13. Utilizan
15. Autobús
20. Habla
22. Prefijo para "dos"
23. Artículo (f.)
24. Madre
27. Cincuenta (núm. rom.)

PROFESIONES

HORIZONTALES:

1. La que cuida enfermos
7. De mí
8. Usar la nariz
10. Artículo (f.)
11. Doctor
13. Evadís
14. El que hace los trajes
16. Bajar
17. Yo dono
19. Trabaja

VERTICALES:

1. Trabajadores
2. Conjunción
3. Costurera
4. Artículo definido
5. El que vende relojes
6. Parte de la iglesia
9. Tela fina
11. Pianista, por ejemplo
12. Usar el teléfono
15. Se usa en la pesca
18. Ahora

LAS BEBIDAS

HORIZONTALES:

1. A él
3. Copas
7. Tomabais
8. Opuesto de sí
10. Zumo
11. Una bebida caliente
12. Conjunción
13. Mojar
16. Bebida de alcohol
17. Se usa para hacer vino
18. Ahora
20. Pronombre
22. Aunque
24. Muy frío

VERTICALES:

1. Menos alto
2. A Ud.
3. Hecho de uvas
4. Autores (abrev.)
5. Falta de
6. Animal peludo
9. Estará
11. Jícaras
13. Nata
14. Avenida (abrev.)
15. Jurisprudencia
16. Bebida caliente
17. Artículo indefinido
21. Editor (abrev.)
23. Idem (abrev.)

MUCHAS NUMERACIONES

1	2	3	4		5	6	7	8
		9			10			
				11			12	
					13	14		15
16			17		18			
		19					20	
21						22		
					23			24
25					26			

HORIZONTALES:

1. Después de undécimo
9. Centímetro (abrev.)
10. Una flor
11. Sobre
12. Cincuenta (núm. rom.)
13. Cada uno (abrev.)
16. Uno más (2 palabras)
18. Cinco menos cuatro
19. Pronombre
20. Centilitro (abrev.)
21. Veinte y veinte
23. Dos y uno
25. Diez y uno
26. Prefijo: la atmósfera

VERTICALES:

1. Catorce y cuatro
   (ortografía poco usada)
2. Uranio (abrev.)
3. Cincuenta y treinta
4. Decámetro (abrev.)
5. Treinta y veinte
6. Andar
7. Cuatrocientos y
   seiscientos
8. Pronombre
14. Diez menos nueve
15. Julián (abrev.)
17. Escuchar
20. Bajar
22. Prefijo: tres
24. Abajo

LA FIESTA

HORIZONTALES:

1. Detención
6. Conjunción negativa
7. Grupo de músicos
9. Doce meses
11. Desde
12. Cuesta
14. Hacia
16. Otrosí (latín)
17. Tarde (abrev.)
18. Con tal que
19. Donas
20. Agradable
22. Uranio (abrev.)
23. Sur (abrev.)
24. Máscara
28. Desde
29. A el
30. Anda

VERTICALES:

1. Olla decorada
2. Abreviación (abrev.)
3. Dona
4. Va
5. Verbo auxiliar
6. Cumpleaños de Cristo
8. Desde
10. ¡ Bravo! (pl.)
13. Estado Mayor (abrev.)
15. Festividad
17. Pronombre (2.° pers.)
18. Su casa (abrev.)
20. Cubre con oro
21. Lámpara
25. Idem (latín) (abrev.)
26. Conozco
27. A el

EL PERIODICO

HORIZONTALES:

1. Diario
8. Desde
9. Andarás
10. Impresor
12. Acompaña el catarro
14. Algo con que se ve
15. Tarde (abrev.)
16. Escritora
18. Afirmativo
19. Conozco
20. Este (abrev.)
21. Anécdota verídica
24. Individuo
25. Agosto (abrev.)
26. Conjunción

VERTICALES:

2. Editorial (abrev.)
3. Escritor de prensa
4. Escriba en el sobre
5. Andará
6. Bebida caliente
7. Animal peludo
10. Tarde (abrev.)
11. Pronombre
13. Dona
14. Fiesta escandalosa
15. Clase, especie
17. Utilizan
20. Estados Unidos
    (abrev.)
22. Centigramo (abrev.)
23. Pronombre

PAISES DEL MUNDO

HORIZONTALES:

1. País de Centro América
7. Colonia (abrev.)
8. País de Africa
10. Caverna
11. Aquella
13. Van
14. Continente más grande en el mundo
17. Copenhague está allí
21. Ese hombre

VERTICALES:

2. País de América del Sur
3. Madrid está allí
4. Agradable
5. Pronombre
6. Berlín está allí
8. Estados Unidos (abrev.)
9. Cuatro (núm. rom.)
10. País al norte de los E.U.
12. América del Sur en inglés (abrev.)
15. Opuesto de no
16. Autores (abrev.)
18. Pronombre
19. A el
20. Centro América (abrev.)

EL JARDINERO

HORIZONTALES:

1. Huerta
7. También
8. Maleza que tiene flores amarillas
11. Poda
12. Una clase de árbol
13. Terminación de un verbo
14. Ahora
15. Conjunción
17. Flor amarilla
20. Pronombre
21. Renuevo, ramo tierno

VERTICALES:

1. Hortelano
2. Querer
3. Vástago
4. Medicina
5. No saber
6. No existe (2 palabras)
9. América del Norte (abrev.)
10. Una parte de la flor
14. También
16. Flor que crece en el árbol
18. Apéndice de pájaro
19. Segovia (abrev.)

LETREROS DEL CAMINO

	1		2			3		4
5			6					
	7	8						9
10							11	
12		13	14	15	16		17	
	18					19		
20					21		22	
		23	24				25	
	26			27	28			

HORIZONTALES:

1. Mecedora
5. Negativo
6. Hacia
7. Apartadero
10. Ultimo día de la semana (abrev.)
11. Pronombre
12. Venadio (abrev.)
13. Pasillo
17. Andar
18. Modo de salir
20. Quinientos y quinientos
21. Salón de clases
23. Pronombre
25. Editor (abrev.)
26. Lento

VERTICALES:

1. Curva
2. Plural de "la"
3. Beneficio
4. Conjunción
8. Intersección
9. No abierto
10. Desviación (abrev.)
11. Pronombre (obj.)
14. A el
15. Opuesto de no
16. Poema
18. Aunque
19. Oro (símbolo)
20. Pronombre (obj.)
22. Vi un libro
24. Está
27. Pregunta (abrev.)
28. Area (abrev.)

FOTOGRAFIA

HORIZONTALES:

1. Cinta
7. Enero, por ejemplo
8. Bebida (hecha en Puerto Rico)
9. Estar
11. Eché una mirada
12. Imitación
13. Se usa para pescar
14. Avenida (abrev.)
15. Limpio y puro
16. Películas reveladas
18. ¡Bravo!
19. Está
20. También
21. A el
23. El que usa la cámara fotográfica

VERTICALES:

1. Moneda de México
2. Moneda pagado (2 palabras)
3. Andar
4. Preposición
5. Artículo indefinido
6. Sulfúrico y nítrico, p. ej.
10. Competidor
11. Vedas
12. Cinematógrafo
13. Desarrolla la película
15. Conjunción
17. Una bebida caliente
20. Mí mismo
21. Terminación de verbos
22. Artículo neutro
24. Conjunción

English — Spanish
Vocabulary

— A —

accuse — acusar
accustomed — soler
afternoon — tarde (abr.: T.)
air — aire
all — todas
alone — solo
altar — ara
and — y
animals — animales
apple — manzana
are — son
artist — artista
at — en
auburn — castaño
August — agosto (abr.: ag.)
aunt — tía
autumn — otoño
avalanche — alud
avenue — avenida (abr.: Av.)
axle — eje

— B —

bank — banco
B. C. — A. C. (antes de Cristo)
be — estar, ser
bear — osa, oso
believe — creo, creí
bind (tie) — ato
bishop — obispo (abr.: Ob.)
blouse — blusa
body — botas
brake — freno
brook — arroyo

bull — toro
business — negocio
business affairs — asuntos
buy — compran

— C —

cabbage — col
calendar — almanaque
cars — autos
cat — gato
celery — apio
chair — silla
check — cheque
cheeks — mejillas
chord — cuerdas
city — ciudad
clear soup — sopa clara
climate — clima
cloak — manto
clothing — vestido
colors — colores
couch — sofá
count — contar
credit — crédito

— D —

dawn — alba
December — diciembre (abr.: dic.)
decoration — ornato
diamonds — oros
dining rooms — comedores
ditto — ídem (abr.: id.)
dollar — dólar
donkey — burro
dress, suit — traje

— E —

ears — orejas
eat — comes
echo — eco
elbow — codo
eleven — once
emerald — esmeralda
enclose — cercar
engine — motor
epoch, age — era
equal, tie — empatar
estuary — ría
eye — ojo
eyelash — pestaña

— F —

faith — fe
fall — caer
family — familia
farce — farsa
fig — higo
fog — niebla
food — comida
four — cuatro (núm. rom.: IV)
fourteen — catorce
fowl — ave
from — de

— G —

garage — garaje
garden — jardín
give — dar, doy, das, da, dan, di,
go — ir, voy, va, van,
gold — oro
grape — uva
gray — gris
green — verde
green pepper — ají
gulf — golfo

— H —

hair — pelo
half — mitad
handle — asa
have — he, ha
he — él
head — cabeza
hear — oír, oí
heart — corazón
here — acá
horse — caballo
house — casa
hundred — cien, cientos
hyancinth — jacinto

— I —

I — yo
if — si
important (to be) — importar
in — en
infinitive ending — ar
inherit — adir
irregular verbs — verbos irreg.
is — es
it — lo

— J —

juice — jugo

— K —

know — sé

— L —

lake — lago
lamb — cordero
lamp — lámpara
laugh — ría, rías, rían
lawn — prado

let — dejas
light — luz
lip — labio
long — largo

— M —

machine — máquina
maple tree — arce
me — mí
milligram — miligramo (abr.: mg.)
Monday — lunes
month — mes
more — más
mouth — boca
musicians — músicos
my — mis

— N —

negative — no
neither, nor — ni
ninety — noventa
ninth — noveno
nose — nariz
now, already — ya
numbers — números

— O —

objective pronoun — me, ti, os
ocean — océano
odd (uneven) — non
on — en
one — un, una, uno
oneself — se
open — abrir
opera — ópera
or — o
orange — naranja
order — orden

others — otros
ox less than two years old — eral

— P —

pay — pagar
perhaps — acaso
plate — plato
plural ending — es
post office — correo
postscript — posdata (abr., pd.)
praise — loa, loan
pray — ora
promenade, walk — paseo

— R —

rain — lluvia
rake — rastro
read — leer, leí
rich — rico
road — camino
roast — asado
roast (verb) — asar, asan
root — raíz
R. R. (railroad) — F. C. (ferro-carril)

— S —

sales slip — vale
Saturday — sábado
sauce — salsa
say — decir, dicen, diría
season — estación
see — veo, veas, ve
shares — lotes
she — ella
sheaf — haz
shovel — pala
shrimp — camarón

six — seis
sixty — sesenta
sky — cielo
sleeve — manga
snow — nieve
so — así
South America — América
  del Sur
speak — hablar
station — etapa
store — tienda
street lamp — farol
stroke — rasgo
such — tal
support — basar

— T —

tall — alto
that — ese, esa, eso
the — el, la, las, los
theater — teatro
there — allí
there is, are — hay
thirteen — trece
this — este, esta, esto
thousand — mil
Thursday — jueves
tie (equal score) — empatar
to — a
today — hoy
to him (her, you) — le
to the — a la, a el (al)
town — pueblo
tracks — rastros
tub — tina
Tuesday — martes
twelfth — doce
twentieth — vigésimo
twenty-two — veintidós

— U —

under — so
unite — unir
us — nos
use — usar, usan, use
useful — útil
usher — ujier

— V —

ventilation — oreo
vest — chaleco

— W —

was — era
water — agua
weather — tiempo
Wednesday — miércoles
weight — pesa
well — bien
whether — ora
white — blanco
wing — ala
winter — invierno
without — sin
worth — vale

— Y —

yacht — yate
yellow — amarillo
yes — sí
you — tú, ti, os, su
your — su, sus
Your Holiness — Su Santidad

— Z —

zero — cero (0)

Vocabulario

Español — Inglés

— A —

a — to, at
abajo — under
abierto — open
abril — April
abrir — to open
acompaña el catarro, — accompanies a cold   tos, cough
acosar — to beset
adicional — more
adulto — adult
a el - al — to the
a ella — to her
a ellos - (les) — to them
afirmativo — yes
afligir — to ail
ágil — spry
agosto — August
agradable — pleasant; agradable — sweet; acogedor — kindly, welcoming
agua — water
agüero — omen
aguja — needle
ahora — now, already
ahorro — economy
alabar — to praise
Alférez — Ensign
alfombra — rug
algo - cosa — something, thing
alguno — some
allende — beyond
almirante — admiral
altura — altitude
amarillento — yellowish
ambas Américas — both Americas
América del Norte — North America

ambulancia — ambulance
analizar — test
andar — to go, walk
anécdota verídica — true story
anillo — ring
animal peludo — hairy animal
antes del mediodia — before noon
antiaéreo — anti-aircraft
aparejo — gear, equipment
Apartado Aéreo — post-office box
aparte — paragraph
apuesta — bet
aquella — that
arado — plow
árbol — tree
área — area
arena — sand
armada — navy
arriba — up
arsenal — shipyard
ascensor — elevator
asi — so
astropiloto — astronaut
asueto — holiday
ata — tie; bind
atún — tuna
aunque — if
autobús — bus
a Vdes. (ustedes) — to you, pl.
avena — oats
avenida — avenue
aviación — aviation
aviador — pilot
avión — airplane; de retro-propulsión — astrojet
aviso — notice

— B —

bajar — fall
baño — tub
barco — ship
barquero — boatman
bebe o come — drink or eat
bebida — drink

beneficio — profit
bien cocido — well done; done
billete — ticket
blanco — blank
blando — soft

boda — wedding
bonito — pretty
borde — edge; de ataque — leading edge
bote — boat

brisa — breeze
broca — reel
buena — fine, good
bulbo — bulb
burro — donkey

— C —

caballo — horse
cada — every
cadera — hip
caliente — hot
calle — street
cama — bed
camilla — stretcher
canario — canary
canasta — basket
canción — song
carbón — coal
cargo de — care of
carrete — reel
carta — letter
cartero — postman
casa — house
casualidades — accidents
catre — cot
caverna — cave
cebra — zebra
ceniza — ash
centeno — rye
Centro América — Central America
cercena — cut, clip
cerdo — pork
ceremonia — ceremony
cerro pequeño — small hill
cervato — fawn
césped — lawn
cielo — sky
cifra — figure
cine — movies
cinta — film
citó — cited

ciudad — city
clase — type
coche de trole — trolley
cohete — rocket
color — color
combustible — gas
como — as
cómo — how
compañia — company
compás del marinero — seaman's compass
competidor — rival
conozco - sé — I know
con prioridad — before
contador público — Certified Public Accountant
con tal que — provided that
copa — drink containers
corazón — heart
correo — Post Office
correr — to run
corriente — current
corta — cut, slip
cosa — thing
coser — to sew
costa — cost
costilla — rib
costumbres — customs
costurera — dressmaker
cráneo — skull
cronómetro — clock
cuenta — account
cultivar — to farm
curar — to cure

— D —

de — from; of
deber — to owe
debido — owed
décimo — tenth
decir — to say; utter
dedo del pie — toe
de ella — her

de esta manera — this way
dejar — to let; allow
de mi - mi, mis — my
dentista — dentist
dentro de — in; inside of
denuncia — accusation

deporte — sport
depresión — dip
desarrolla la película — develops the film
desatar — to undo; untie
descubrimiento — discovery
desde - de — from
destrucción — ruin
de usted — your

diario — daily paper
diez — ten
doce meses — 12 months
doce pulgadas — 12 inches
donar — to give
donde — where
dos — two
duplicado — duplicate

— E —

eché una mirada — I took a look
edad — age
él — he; ella — she
el día antes de hoy — day before today
elefantes — elephants
elevar — to hoist
ella se lustra las uñas — she polishes her nails
el que — one who
en — at; in; on
enchapa con oro — plate with gold
en descubierto — overdrawn
enero — January
en este lugar — in this place
enfado — anger
enfermera — nurse
enjuagar — to rinse
entrada — entry
envase para vino — wine bag
epístola — letter
equipo — rig; equipment
erecto — erect
es — is
escoria — slag
escriba en el sobre — write on the envelope
escritora — writer
escritor de prensa — reporter
escritorio — desk
escuchar — to hear
escuela — school
ese hombre — that man
esa tarde — that afternoon, evening
espía — spy
está — is
estado mayor — general staff
Estados Unidos — United States
estampilla — stamp
están — are
estaño — tin
este — east
estenordeste — east-northeast
estesudeste — east-southeast
estrella — star
estuario — estuary
estudiante — student
evadir — to elude
excursión — trip
existir — to be
explosivo — explosive

— F —

fábrica — make
falto de — short of
felpudo — mat
fermenta — brews
ferrocarril — railroad
festividad — fiesta
fiesta escandalosa — scandalous party
finalidad — finality

finca — estate
flor — flower
flor amarilla — yellow flower
francés — French
franqueo — postage
fricción — massage
fruta de la higuera — fig tree
fuego — fire
fuera — out

fuerte — strong
funcionario público — notary

fundamento — basis
fusible — fuse

— G —

galón — gallon
ganadero — cattleman
ganó — won
garantía — guarantee
garfio — fishhook
gira en el viento — whirls in the wind

giro postal — money order
gordo — fat
granada — grenade
grupo de músicos — band
guarda — tends; guards
guarida — den

— H —

hablar — to speak
hacer — to make; do
hacer crespo el pelo — make the hair curly
hacha — ax
hacia — toward
hecho — made
hecho de roble — made of oak
hecho de uvas — made from grapes
hecho para beneficio — done for profit
herido — hurt
hermana — sister
héroe — hero
herraje de sillero — saddlery

hielo que se forma — ice that forms
hiena — hyena
hierba — grass
hierro — iron
hija — daughter
hijo — son
hogar — fireplace
hojas — leaves
hombre — man
hombre que pesca — man who fishes
hombre valiente — brave man
hormiga — ant
hortelano — gardener
huerta — vegetable garden

— I —

idem — ditto (Latin)
idiota — idiot
imitación — copy
imitar — to imitate
imperativo de raer — order to erase

impresor — printer
incendiar — to burn
inhábil — unable
intersección — junction
ir — to go
izquierda — left

— J —

ija! — ha!
jamás — never
jícara — cup
ijo! — ho!
joven — young

juego — game
jugar — to play
juguete — toy
julio — July
jurisprudencia — law

— L —

lámpara — light
lápiz — pencil
lateral — side
leer — to read
lento — slow
leopardo — leopard
libro — book
limón — lemon

lirio — lily
liso — even; flat
litro — liter
lo — it
locomotoro — train
lodo — mud
luna — moon
luz — light

— LL —

llamar — to call
lleno — full

llevar — to lead
lluvia — rain

— M —

madre — mother
maestro — teacher
maleta — bag, suitcase
maleza que tiene flores amarillas — weed that has yellow flowers
manera de pescar — way to fish
manzana — block of houses
mapache — coon
máquina de volar — flying machine
marca tiempo — keeps time
marea — tide
margen — rim
marido — husband
más — more
máscara — mask
más o menos — more or less
material sintético — synthetic material
Mayo — May
mayor — senior
mazorca — ear (of corn)

media — stocking
médico — doctor
mediodía — noon
mejicano — Mexican
menos — less
meta — goal
mi — my
mí mismo — me myself
mineral en bruto — ore
mirar — to look
modo — mode
modo de salir — way to leave
mojado — wet
mojar — to soak, drench
montaña — mountain
montón de heno — a haystack
muchacho — child
mucho — much
mueble — piece of furniture
mundo — world
muñeca — doll
musgo — moss

— N —

nada — no
narciso — daffodil
nariz — nose

nativo de Tejas — native of Texas
nata — cream
natación — swimming

negocio — deal
nieve — snow
ninguno — none
niño — boy, baby
no — not
noche — night
no más — no more

nordeste — northeast
nornordeste — north-northeast
nos — us; **nosotros** — we, us
novia — bride; **novio** — groom
nuestro — our
número — number

— O —

o — or
obedecer — to obey
obispo — bishop
obrar — to work
obtener — to get
océano — ocean
ochenta — eighty
oeste — west
ojo — eye
óleo — oil
olla decorada — decorated pot
olor — odor

orden — order
orden de — order of
oreja — ear
oriente — east
oro — gold
osar — to dare
otra clase de árbol — another
  kind of tree
otro — other
otrosí — item
oveja — female sheep, ewe
oxígeno — oxygen

— P —

padre — father
paga — pays; **pagado** — paid
país — country
palabra usada para espantar —
  word used to frighten
palanca — lever
pantera — panther
paradero del tren — depot
para planchar ropa — for ironing
  clothes
parecer — to seem
pasado — past
pasillo — passage way
paso — step
peinado — hair dressing
películas reveladas — devel-
  oped films
peor — worse
perder — lose; **pérdida** — loss
pero — but
pescar — to fish
pianista — pianist

pierna — leg
pino — pine
plata — silver
plomo — lead
pluma — pen
plural — plural
poda — trim, prune
poema — ode
por — by, for; **por ejemplo**
  p. ej.) — for example; **por**
  otra parte — on the other hand
porte pagado — postage paid
precio — price
pregunta — question
primer mes del año — first
  month of the year
pronombre — pronoun
pronto — quickly
protagonista — hero
provechoso — useful
pueblo — town
punto — dot

— Q —

querer — to love

— R —

ráfaga — burst from automatic
weapon
raíz — root
rancho — ranch
raro — rare
rayo — ray
recibí — received
red — net
reloj — watch, clock

remo — oar
revendió — resold
Reverendo — Reverend
rico — rich
riñón — kidney
rodeo — detour, go-around
rojo — red; **rojo pálido** — pale
red
rostro — face

— S —

sábado — Saturday
saber — to know
salvo error — errors excepted
sangre — blood
santo — Saint
Sargento — Sergeant
sastre — tailor
secoya — redwood
secretaría — office of the secre-
tary
seguido — continued
seis — six
semestre — term
Señor — Mister
sentir — to feel
ser — to be
sesión — session
se usa en la pesca — used in
fishing
sexto — sixth
si — if
sí — yes
siempre verdes — evergreens

siete — seven
signo — mark
silla — chair
sobre — on, over; onto
sobres — envelopes
¡socorro! — help!
sofá — settee
solamente — only
soldado — soldier
sonido de la vaca — sound of a
cow
sonó — rang
sotavento — leeward; lee
suburbio — suburb
su casa — your house
suceso — event
sudeste — southeast
sudoeste — southwest
suela de un zapato — sole of a
shoe
sur — south
sustituto — substitute

— T —

tal — such
taladro — drill
tallo — stem
también — also, too
tanque — tank
tanza — fishline
tarde — afternoon
tela fina — fine material
tempestuoso — stormy
tener — to own; have, tengo —
  I have
Teniente — Lieutenant
tenis — tennis
terminación — ending

tienda — store
tierra — earth
tímido — shy
tinte — dye
tío — uncle
tos — cough
trabajo — work
tratar — to try
treinta — thirty
trenza — braid, plait
triste — sad
tropas — Army
trota — trot

— U —

último día de la semana — last
  day of the week
ultra — ultra

usar — to use
usted - Ud., ustedes - Uds. — you
utilizan — use

— V —

vaca — cow
vacaciones — vacations
va con pimienta — goes with
  pepper
vagabundo — vagabond
vago — bum
vara — pole
vástago — twig, branch
veda — veto
vela — sail
venta — sale
ver — to see

verdadero — real
verde — green
veterano — veteran
veterinario — veterinary (vet)
vía — road
viejo — old
víspera — eve
visto — seen
voy — I go
vuelta completa de la pista —
  complete revolution of the
  track, lap

— Z —

zapatería — shoe store
zarpar — to sail

zumo — juice

ANSWER KEY

NUMBERS *(page 4)* **Horizontales:** *1. catorce; 6. unir; 7. él; 9. caer; 10. noveno; 13. ave; 16. sesenta.* **Verticales:** *1. cientos; 2. tú; 3. once; 4. rían; 5. creo; 8. lo; 11. veas; 12. una; 14. ve; 15. en.*

INFINITIVES *(page 5)* **Horizontales:** *1. hablar; 6. caer; 8. use; 9. asar; 10. ir; 11. dar; 13. ir; 14. abrir.* **Verticales:** *2. acusar; 3. basar; 4. leer; 5. ar; 7. cercar; 9. adir; 12. oír.*

WATER *(page 6)* **Horizontales:** *3. lo; 4. océano; 8. las rías; 10. fe; 11. no; 12. oreo; 13. yate; 15. lago; 16. ir.* **Verticales:** *1. golfo; 2. mes; 3. loan; 5. caer; 6. arroyo; 7. ni; 9. soler; 14. ti.*

MORE NUMBERS *(page 7)* **Horizontales:** *1. veintidós; 5. un; 6. doce; 7. este; 9. de; 10. uno; 12. id.; 14. treces; 16. mitad; 17. o; 18. mil; 20. cien; 21. oro.* **Verticales:** *1. vigésimo; 2. noventa; 3. duodécimo; 4. once; 8. tú; 11. orden; 13. di; 15. solo; 19. ir.*

ANIMALS *(page 8)* **Horizontales:** *1. caballo; 5. rasgo; 7. dar; 9. eco; 10. ato; 12. rastros; 13. asa.* **Verticales:** *1. cordero; 2. burros; 3. las; 4. ojo; 6. gatos; 8. acá; 10. ara; 11. osa.*

THE CALENDAR *(page 9)* **Horizontales:** *1. miércoles; 7. una; 8. tía; 9. eje; 11. sus; 12. seis; 13. so; 14. veo; 16. invierno; 19. P.D.; 20. S.A.* **Verticales:** *1. martes; 2. estación; 3. comes; 4. lunes; 5. en; 6. sábado; 10. jueves; 13. son; 15. era; 16. id.; 17. va; 18. Ob.*

COLORS *(page 10)* **Horizontales:** *1. naranja; 5. ve; 7. acá; 10. esmeralda; 14. gris; 15. en; 16. de; 18. alto; 20. es; 21. largo; 22. otoño; 24. así; 25. oso.* **Verticales:** *2. ag.; 3. amarillo; 4. blanco; 5. verde; 6. es; 8. castaño; 9. al; 11. mg.; 12. era; 13. de; 17. es; 19. oros; 22. os; 23. ti.*

FOOD *(page 11)* **Horizontales:** *1. comedores; 6. asar; 7. naranja; 9. rías; 12. higo; 13. ornato; 14. o; 15. al; 16. yo; 19. el; 21. sopa clara.* **Verticales:** *1. camarones; 2. os; 3. manzana; 4. era; 5. osa; 8. jugo; 10. ir; 11. salsa; 12. hoy; 17. ora; 18. uva; 20. lo.*

AT THE BANK *(page 12)* **Horizontales:** *1. crédito; 7. toros; 8. eral; 9. pagar; 11. usar; 13. sí; 14. es; 16. banco.* **Verticales:** *1. cheques; 2. etapa; 3. dólar; 4. ir; 5. todas; 6. os; 10. rico; 12. S.S.; 15. en.*

IRREGULAR VERBS *(page 13)* **Horizontales:** *1. he; 2. ve; 5. das; 6. contar; 8. hay; 9. así; 10. ría; 11. creí; 13. oí.* **Verticales:** *1. ha; 2. van; 3. estar; 4. diría; 5. doy; 6. caer; 7. así; 12. ir.*

BUSINESS *(page 14)* **Horizontales:** *1. crédito; 6. mis; 7. mil; 9. prado; 12. arce;*

14. *asuntos;* 17. *non;* 18. *ala.* **Verticales:** 1. *compran;* 2. *ella;* 3. *importa;* 4. *ti;* 5. *os;* 8. *ir;* 10. *dan;* 11. *pesa;* 13. *col;* 15. *so;* 16. *un.*

THE GARDEN *(page 15)* **Horizontales:** 1. *jardín;* 5. *pala;* 6. *acaso;* 8. *si;* 9. *da;* 10. *en;* 11. *raíz;* 13. *otros;* 14. *o;* 15. *sin.* **Verticales:** 1. *jacinto;* 2. *a la;* 3. *rastros;* 4. *id.;* 5. *paseo;* 7. *haz;* 9. *di;* 12. *así.*

THE OPERA *(page 16)* **Horizontales:** 1. *me;* 3. *tina;* 6. *ujier;* 7. *sé;* 8. *sí;* 9. *cuerdas;* 12. *o;* 13. *loa;* 14. *su;* 15. *ha.* **Verticales:** 1. *músicos;* 2. *eje;* 3. *teatros;* 4. *ir;* 5. *artista;* 8. *S.A.;* 10. *él;* 11. *da.*

MACHINES *(page 17)* **Horizontales:** 1. *garajes;* 4. *máquina;* 7. *av.;* 8. *tú;* 9. *freno;* 12. *nos.* **Verticales:** 2. *a la;* 3. *agua;* 4. *motor;* 5. *IV;* 6. *autos;* 9. *F.C.;* 10. *en;* 11. *no.*

LA ESCUELA *(page 18)* **Horizontales:** 1. *school;* 5. *up;* 7. *horse;* 9. *Utah;* 12. *seen;* 13. *dare;* 14. *S.A.;* 15. *entry;* 16. *deal;* 18. *teachers;* 20. *books.* **Verticales:** 1. *student;* 2. *heart;* 3. *oh;* 4. *loss;* 5. *use;* 6. *pencil;* 8. *reader;* 10. *tan;* 11. *her;* 16. *desk;* 17. *ask;* 19. *ed.*

DENTRO DE LA CASA *(page 19)* **Horizontales:** 1. *furniture;* 7. *is;* 8. *fuse;* 10. *beds;* 12. *rugs;* 14. *we;* 15. *price;* 17. *cot;* 18. *light;* 19. *lot;* 20. *A.C.;* 21. *mode;* 22. *chair;* 25. *St.;* 26. *sky.* **Verticales:** 1. *fireplace;* 2. *us;* 3. *if;* 4. *tubs;* 5. *use;* 6. *redwood;* 9. *such;* 11. *settee;* 12. *rig;* 13. *get;* 16. *rich;* 17. *clock;* 23. *as;* 24. *it.*

NUMEROS *(page 20)* **Horizontales:** 1. *fifty-four;* 7. *on;* 8. *it;* 9. *eighty;* 10. *teen;* 11. *thirty;* 13. *only;* 15. *no;* 16. *sevens;* 18. *VI;* 19. *th;* 20. *sixth;* 21. *he.* **Verticales:** 1. *forty-one;* 2. *in;* 3. *twenty-six;* 4. *fig.;* 5. *other;* 6. *ray;* 12. *tenth;* 14. *no;* 17. *she;* 18. *VI.*

ADJETIVOS *(page 21)* **Horizontales:** 1. *pretty;* 5. *old;* 6. *seven;* 8. *noon;* 9. *S.A.;* 11. *get;* 13. *easier;* 14. *ant;* 15. *wet;* 16. *strong;* 19. *or.* **Verticales:** 1. *pleasant;* 2. *even;* 3. *young;* 4. *adult;* 7. *none;* 10. *astro;* 12. *every;* 13. *east;* 17. *or;* 18. *go.*

EL CUERPO *(page 22)* **Horizontales:** 1. *shoulders;* 9. *kidney;* 10. *it;* 11. *up;* 12. *age;* 13. *be;* 15. *lullaby;* 19. *toe;* 20. *left;* 22. *it's;* 23. *nose;* 24. *seem;* 26. *doll.* **Verticales:** 1. *skull;* 2. *hip;* 3. *o.d.;* 4. *unable;* 5. *leg;* 6. *dye;* 7. *rib;* 8. *step;* 14. *eyes;* 16. *utter;* 17. *lose;* 18. *blood;* 21. *feel;* 22. *is;* 25. *my.*

EL TIEMPO *(page 23)* **Horizontales:** 1. *sunshine;* 6. *to;* 7. *Na;* 9. *louder;* 11. *worse;* 12. *of;* 14. *omen;* 15. *sky;* 17. *rain;* 20. *moon;* 21. *ire;* 22. *SW;* 23. *let.* **Verticales:** 1. *so;* 2. *stormy;* 3. *house;* 4. *NNE;* 5. *earth;* 8. *cloud;* 9. *look;* 10. *den;* 13. *F.;* 15. *snow;* 16. *mire;* 18. *ail;* 19. *net;* 20. *ms.*

EL CORREO *(page 24)* **Horizontales:** 1. *gas;* 4. *red;* 6. *postmen;* 7. *M.O.;* 8. *Ave.;* 9. *ash;* 10. *made;* 11. *it;* 12. *up;* 13. *lawn;* 14. *from;* 16. *C.P.A.;* 18. *P.O.;* 19. *be;* 20. *letter;* 21. *ten;* 22. *SE.* **Verticales:** 1. *go;* 2. *as;* 3. *stamp;* 4. *read;* 5. *envelopes;* 6. *postage;* 7. *mail;* 12. *uncle;* 14. *fat;* 15. *more;* 17. *pen;* 19. *by.*

VERDE *(page 25)* **Horizontales:** 1. *green;* 4. *tree;* 6. *lead;* 7. *moss;* 10. *Ens.;* 11. *oar;* 12. *spry;* 14. *or;* 15. *VI;* 18. *event;* 21. *seven;* 22. *owe;* 24. *estate.* **Verticales:** 1. *grass;* 2. *red;* 3. *E.E.;* 4. *ten;* 5. *as;* 6. *leaves;* 7. *May;* 8. *or;* 9. *spruce;* 11. *or;* 13. *pines;* 16. *I've;* 17. *root;* 19. *eve;* 20. *TNT;* 23. *we.*

EL ASUETO *(page 26)* **Horizontales:** 1. *vacations;* 8. *ago;* 9. *row;* 10. *game;* 11. *ad;* 12. *term;* 13. *brews;* 16. *real;* 18. *bi;* 19. *no;* 21. *it;* 22. *on;* 23. *drill;* 26. *bag;* 27. *fish.* **Verticales:** 1. *vagabonds;* 3. *camper;* 3. *age;* 4. *to;* 5. *order;* 6. *no;* 7. *swimming;* 11. *at;* 14. *we;* 15. *sails;* 17. *Lt.;* 18. *boat;* 20. *or;* 24. *if;* 25. *Ll.*

MEDICO *(page 27)* **Horizontales:** 1. *accidents;* 7. *R.N.;* 8. *it;* 9. *burn;* 11. *doer;* 13. *use;* 14. *rinse;* 15. *cough;* 19. *own;* 20. *cited;* 22. *es;* 23. *doctor.* **Verticales:** 1. *ambulance;* 2. *cure;* 3. *Dr.;* 4. *ending;* 5. *ties;* 6. *stretcher;* 10. *us;* 12. *on;* 15. *cot;* 16. *owed;* 17. *undo;* 18. *hurt;* 21. *is.*

LOS DEPORTES *(page 28)* **Horizontales:** *1. golfing; 6. won; 7. oar; 8. of; 9. pl.; 10. ft.; 11. net; 13. sub.; 14. play; 15. on; 16. troll; 18. son; 19. our; 20. lap; 22. onto; 23. my.* **Verticales:** *1. goal; 2. on; 3. football; 4. no; 5. game; 9. pd.; 10. full; 11. no; 12. tennis; 13. sport; 15. oo; 16. too; 17. run; 18. spy; 21. a.m.*

LA BODA *(page 29)* **Horizontales:** *1. flowers; 6. bride; 8. led; 9. E.S.E.; 11. shy; 12. do; 14. or; 15. ring; 17. man; 18. rim; 19. thing; 21. song; 22. go; 23. we; 24. May.* **Verticales:** *1. Fr.; 2. lily; 3. ode; 4. wedding; 5. rye; 6. baskets; 7. ceremony; 10. so; 13. on; 15. rang; 16. groom; 17. mine; 20. how.*

ANIMALES SALVAJES *(page 30)* **Horizontales:** *1. elephants; 7. oh; 8. coins; 10. up; 11. zoo; 13. S.A.; 14. hyena; 15. tree; 17. bets; 19. odor; 20. so; 21. mat; 23. SOS; 24. out.* **Verticales:** *2. leopard; 3. panther; 4. a.m.; 5. to; 6. shy; 8. customs; 9. done; 11. zebra; 12. oats; 16. eons; 18. soft; 21. my; 22. to.*

AMARILLO *(page 31)* **Horizontales:** *1. discovery; 7. ear; 8. fawn; 9. gal.; 10. be; 11. over; 13. go; 14. do; 15. yellow; 17. it; 18. Bali; 19. lemon; 22. D.D.S.; 23. Sr.; 24. nosy.* **Verticales:** *1. daffodils; 2. sew; 3. canary; 4. or; 5. edge; 6. yellowish; 10. bulb; 12. voter; 13. gold; 16. lady; 20. on; 21. no.*

EL RANCHO *(page 32)* **Horizontales:** *1. cattleman; 8. on; 9. ear; 10. ho; 11. in; 12. oat; 13. saddlery; 15. is; 16. west; 18. P.O.; 19. me; 20. to; 21. ultra; 22. so; 23. ranch; 25. works.* **Verticales:** *1. cows; 2. an; 3. tends; 4. L.A.; 5. er; 6. a haystack; 7. not; 11. idiot; 12. ore; 14. ewe; 17. to; 18. plow; 19. mark; 21. us; 24. as.*

VAMOS DE COMPRAS *(page 33)* **Horizontales:** *1. shoe store; 8. tailor; 9. lemons; 10. Co.; 11. vet.; 12. on; 14. S.A.; 15. sole; 17. at; 18. ade; 19. nylon; 20. er; 21; deal; 22. session.* **Verticales:** *1. stockings; 2. ha; 3. oil; 4. elevators; 5. some; 6. trots; 7. resold; 13. needle; 14. sales; 16. oaken; 21. do.*

LOS PAISES *(page 34)* **Horizontales:** *1. America; 6. try; 7. farm; 10. lee; 11. Brazil; 13. X; 14. VI; 15. Canada; 17. on; 18. Lima; 20. bum; 22. by; 23. an; 24. ape; 25. in.* **Verticales:** *1. Arabia; 2. my; 3. if; 4. call; 5. are; 8. Mexican; 9. Japan; 12. Italy; 15. Cuba; 16. Nome; 19. man; 21. up; 22. be.*

AVIACION *(page 35)* **Horizontales:** *1. airplanes; 6. son; 7. ticket; 8. rare; 10. obey; 12. oxy; 13. jet; 14. an; 16. es; 17. planet; 20. ten; 22. tuna; 23. toy; 24. term.* **Verticales:** *1. astrojet; 2. rocket; 3. astronaut; 4. no; 5. entry; 9. ax; 11. beset; 14. alt; 15. it; 18. NNE; 19. ear; 21. no.*

VAMOS A ARREGLARNOS *(page 36)* **Horizontales:** *1. peluquero; 5. manicura; 9. al; 10. los; 13. ruina; 16. afeitadas; 19. rizar; 20. fina; 21. ir; 22. caer; 23. de.* **Verticales:** *1. pomada; 2. útil; 4. ría; 6. al; 7. corta; 8. usuario; 11. masaje; 12. peine; 14. id.; 15. N.A.; 17. fría, 18. izar; 20. F.C.*

LA FAMILIA *(page 37)* **Horizontales:** *1. padre; 5. tía; 7. ría; 8. ser; 10. ir; 11. plata; 12. me; 13. nos; 15. amo; 16. hijo; 17. baño; 18. lado; 20. cosa; 22. mes; 23. lo; 24. no.* **Verticales:** *1. prima; 2. aire; 3. da; 4. esposo; 5. trabajar; 6. abajo; 9. él; 13. niños; 14. ojos; 16. hace; 19. oro; 21. al.*

LA CIUDAD *(page 38)* **Horizontales:** *1. camino; 7. ver; 9. sí; 11. Sr.; 12. cuadra; 14. a; 15. base; 16. in; 17. ciudad; 18. Av.; 19. son; 21. Ob; 23. loma; 25. ni; 26. plaza.* **Verticales:** *2. Av.; 3. mercado; 4. ir; 5. os; 6. estación; 8. tranvía; 10. raed; 11. sria.; 13. usan; 15. bus; 20. voz; 22. bi; 23. la; 24. ma; 27. L.*

PROFESIONES *(page 39)* **Horizontales:** *1. enfermera; 7. mi; 8. oler; 10. la; 11. médico; 13. eludís; 14. sastre; 16. caer; 17. doy; 19. obra.* **Verticales:** *1. empleados; 2. ni; 3. modista; 4. el; 5. relojero; 6. ara; 9. seda; 11. músico; 12. discar; 15. red; 18. ya.*

LAS BEBIDAS *(page 40)* **Horizontales:** *1. al; 3. vasos; 7. bebíais; 8. no; 10. jugo; 11. té; 12. o; 13. calar; 16. cerveza; 17. uva; 18. ya; 20. me; 22. si; 24. helado.*

Verticales: *1. abajo; 2. le; 3. vino; 4. A.A.; 5. sin; 6. oso; 9. será; 11. tazas; 13. crema; 14. Av.; 15. ley; 16. café; 17. un; 21. ed; 23. id.*

MUCHAS NUMERACIONES *(page 41)* **Horizontales:** *1. duodécimo; 9. cm.; 10. iris; 11. en; 12. L; 13. c/u; 16. y uno; 18. un; 19. ti; 20. cl; 21. cuarenta; 23. tres; 25. once; 26. aero.* **Verticales:** *1. diez y ocho; 2. U; 3. ochenta; 4. Dm.; 5. cincuenta; 6. ir; 7. mil; 8. os; 14. un; 15. Jul.; 17. oír; 20. caer; 22. tre; 24. so.*

LA FIESTA *(page 42)* **Horizontales:** *1. parada; 6. ni; 7. banda; 9. año; 11. de; 12. vale; 14. a; 16. item; 17. t.; 18. si; 19. das; 20. dulce; 22. U.; 23. S.; 24. disfraz; 28. de; 29. al; 30. va.* **Verticales:** *1. piñata; 2. abr.; 3. da; 4. anda; 5. ha; 6. Navidad; 8. de; 10. olés; 13. E.M.; 15. fiesta; 17. tu; 18. s.c.; 20. dora; 21. luz; 25. id.; 26. sé; 27. al.*

EL PERIODICO *(page 43)* **Horizontales:** *1. periódico; 8. de; 9. irás; 10. tipógrafo; 12. tos; 14. ojo; 15. t.; 16. autora; 18. sí; 19. sé; 20. E.; 21. artículo; 24. uno; 25. ag.; 26. o.* **Verticales:** *2. edit; 3. reportero; 4. dirija; 5. irá; 6. café; 7. oso; 10. t.; 11. os; 13. da; 14. orgía; 15. tipo; 17. usan; 20. E.U.; 22. cg.; 23. lo.*

PAISES DEL MUNDO *(page 44)* **Horizontales:** *1. Guatemala; 7. col.; 8. Egipto; 10. cueva; 11. esa; 13. andan; 14. Asia; 17. Dinamarca; 21. él.* **Verticales:** *2. Argentina; 3. España; 4. acogedor; 5. lo; 6. Alemania; 8. E.U.; 9. IV; 10. Canadá; 12. S.A.; 15. sí; 16. A.A.; 18. me; 19. al; 20. C.A.*

EL JARDINERO *(page 45)* **Horizontales:** *1. jardín; 7. y; 8. amargón; 11. ramonea; 12. dragos; 13. ar; 14. ya; 15. ni; 17. narciso; 20. le; 21. vástago.* **Verticales:** *1. jardinero; 2. amar; 3. rama; 4. droga; 5. ignorar; 6. no es; 9. N.A.; 10. pétalo; 14. y; 16. lila; 18. a la; 19. Seg.*

LETREROS DEL CAMINO *(page 46)* **Horizontales:** *1. columpio; 5. no; 6. a; 7. desvío; 10. dom.; 11. te; 12. V.; 13. paso; 17. ir; 18. salida; 20. mil; 21. aula; 23. me; 25. ed; 26. despacio.* **Verticales:** *1. codo; 2. las; 3. pro; 4. o; 8. empalme; 9. cerrado; 10. dv.; 11. ti; 14. al; 15. sí; 16. oda; 18. si; 19. Au; 20. mi; 22. leí; 24. es; 27. P.; 28. a.*

FOTOGRAFIA *(page 47)* **Horizontales:** *1. película; 7. mes; 8. ron; 9. ser; 11. vi; 12. copia; 13. red; 14. Av.; 15. neto; 16. negativos; 18. olé; 19. es; 20. y; 21. al; 23. fotógrafo.* **Verticales:** *1. peso; 2. ese pago; 3. ir; 4. con; 5. un; 6. ácidos; 10. rival; 11. vetos; 12. cine; 13. revela; 15. ni; 17. té; 20. yo; 21. ar; 22. lo; 24. o.*

LANGUAGE AND REFERENCE BOOKS

Dictionaries and References
VOX Spanish and English Dictionaries
Cervantes-Walls Spanish and English Dictionary
Klett German and English Dictionary
NTC's New College French & English Dictionary
NTC's New College Greek & English Dictionary
Zanichelli Italian Dictionary
NTC's Dictionary of German False Cognates
NTC's Dictionary of *Faux Amis*
NTC's American Idioms Dictionary
NTC's Dictionary of American Slang and
 Colloquial Expressions
Forbidden American English
Essential American Idioms
Contemporary American Slang
Everyday American English Dictionary
Everyday American Phrases in Content
Beginner's Dictionary of American English Usage
NTC's Dictionary of Grammar Terminology
Robin Hyman's Dictionary of Quotations
Guide to Better English Spelling
303 Dumb Spelling Mistakes
NTC's Dictionary of Literary Terms
The Writer's Handbook
NTC's Dictionary of American Spelling
Diccionario Inglés
El Diccionario Básico Norteamericano
British/American Language Dictionary
The French-Speaking World
The Spanish-Speaking World
The French Businessmate
The German Businessmate
The Spanish Businessmate
Guide to Spanish Idioms
Guide to German Idioms
Guide to French Idioms
Au courant
Guide to Correspondence in Spanish
Guide to Correspondence in French
Español para los Hispanos
Business Russian
Yes! You Can Learn a Foreign Language
Japanese in Plain English
Korean in Plain English
Easy Chinese Phrasebook and Dictionary
Japan Today!
Everything Japanese
Easy Hiragana
Easy Katakana
Easy Kana Workbook

Picture Dictionaries
English; French; Spanish; German

Let's Learn...Picture Dictionaries
English, Spanish, French, German, Italian

Verb References
Complete Handbook of Spanish Verbs
Complete Handbook of Russian Verbs
Spanish Verb Drills
French Verb Drills
German Verb Drills

Grammar References
Spanish Verbs and Essentials of Grammar
Nice 'n Easy Spanish Grammar
French Verbs and Essentials of Grammar
Nice 'n Easy French Grammar
German Verbs and Essentials of Grammar
Nice 'n Easy German Grammar
Italian Verbs and Essentials of Grammar
Essentials of Russian Grammar
Essentials of English Grammar
Roots of the Russian Language

Reading and Translating Contemporary Russian
Essentials of Latin Grammar
Swedish Verbs and Essentials of Grammar

Welcome to...Books
Spain, France, Ancient Greece, Ancient Rome

Language Programs: Audio and Video
Just Listen 'n Learn: Spanish, French, Italian,
 German and Greek
Just Listen 'n Learn PLUS: Spanish, French,
 German
Speak French
Speak Spanish
Speak German
Practice & Improve Your...Spanish, French,
 Italian, and German
Practice & Improve Your...Spanish PLUS, French
 PLUS, Italian PLUS and German PLUS
Conversational...in 7 Days: Spanish, French,
 German, Italian, Portuguese, Greek, Russian,
 Japanese, and Thai
Everyday Japanese
Japanese for Children
Nissan's Business Japanese
Contemporary Business Japanese
Basic French Conversation
Basic Spanish Conversation
Everyday Hebrew
VideoPassport in French and Spanish
How to Pronounce Russian Correctly
How to Pronounce Spanish Correctly
How to Pronounce French Correctly
How to Pronounce Italian Correctly
How to Pronounce Japanese Correctly
L'Express: Ainsi va la France
Listen and Say It Right in English
Once Upon a Time in Spanish, French, German
Let's Sing & Learn in French & Spanish

"Just Enough" Phrase Books
Chinese, Dutch, French, German, Greek, Italian,
 Japanese, Portuguese, Russian, Scandinavian,
 Serbo-Croat, Spanish

Language Game and Humor Books
Easy French Vocabulary Games
Easy French Crossword Puzzles
Easy French Word Games and Puzzles
Easy French Grammar Puzzles
Easy Spanish Crossword Puzzles
Easy Spanish Vocabulary Puzzles
Easy French Word Games and Puzzles
Easy French Culture Games
Easy German Crossword Puzzles
Easy Italian Crossword Puzzles
Let's Learn about Series: Italy, France, Germany,
 Spain, America
Let's Learn Coloring Books in Spanish, French,
 German, Italian, and English
My World in...Coloring Books: Spanish, French,
 German and Italian
German à la Cartoon
Spanish à la Cartoon
French à la Cartoon
101 American English Idioms
El Alfabeto
L' Alphabet

Getting Started Books
Introductory language books in Spanish, French,
 German and Italian

Getting to Know...Series
France, Germany, Spain, Italy,
 Mexico, United States

PASSPORT BOOKS
a division of *NTC Publishing Group*
Lincolnwood, Illinois USA